-Ful and -Less, -Er and -Ness

What Is a Suffix?

Suffix:
A word part added to the end of a word or root to change its meaning

-Ful and -Less, -Er, and -Ness

What Is a Suffix?

by Brian P. Cleary

illustrations by Martin Goneau

M MILLBROOK PRESS / MINNEAPOLIS

Suffixes are word parts that are tacked on to a word.

You'll find a suffix at the end of farmer and preferred.

The **E-R** part of farmer speaks of someone who is doing,

like the **baker** who is baking

or the **Viewer** who is **Viewing**.

Names of jobs might end this way,
for certain words, like teacher,

Painter
Teacher
Banker
Skater
Speaker

Driver
Waiter
Preacher

painter, skater,

banker, waiter,

speaker, driver,

preacher.

The root word is the main word,
as in paint
or skate
or teach.

The suffix is the letters that we see in back of each.

Both E-D and I-N-G are suffixes you'll find

in words like danced and dancing,

designing and designed.

T-I-O-N as a suffix
Adds on to an action.

You'll find it in de**letion**,

celebration,

and subtraction.

O-U-S means "full of."

It's a Suffix that can tell us

if people are harmonious
or dangerous or zealous.

F-U-L means "full of" too,
like powerful or truthful,

colorful or painful,

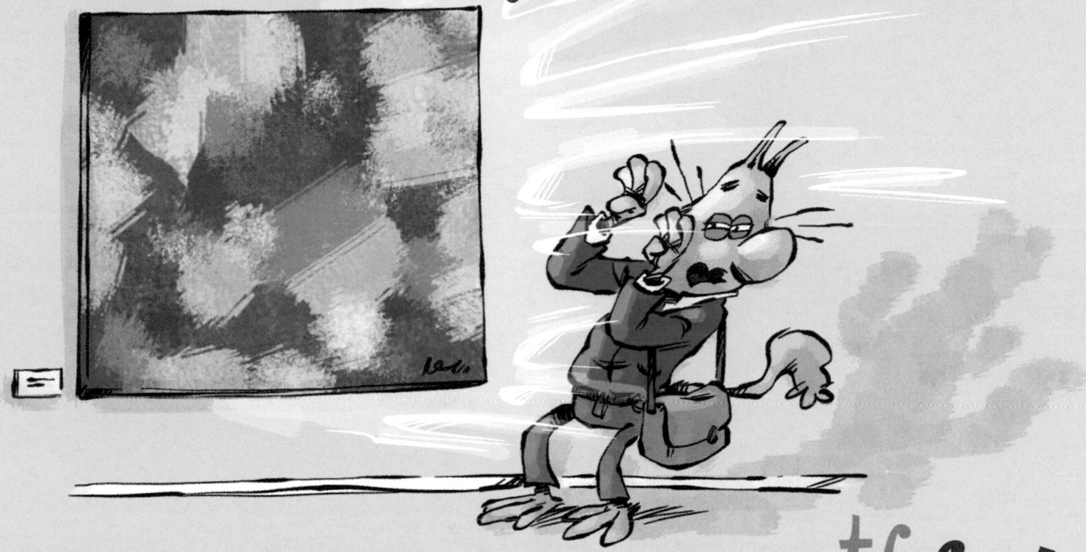

also beautiful and youthful.

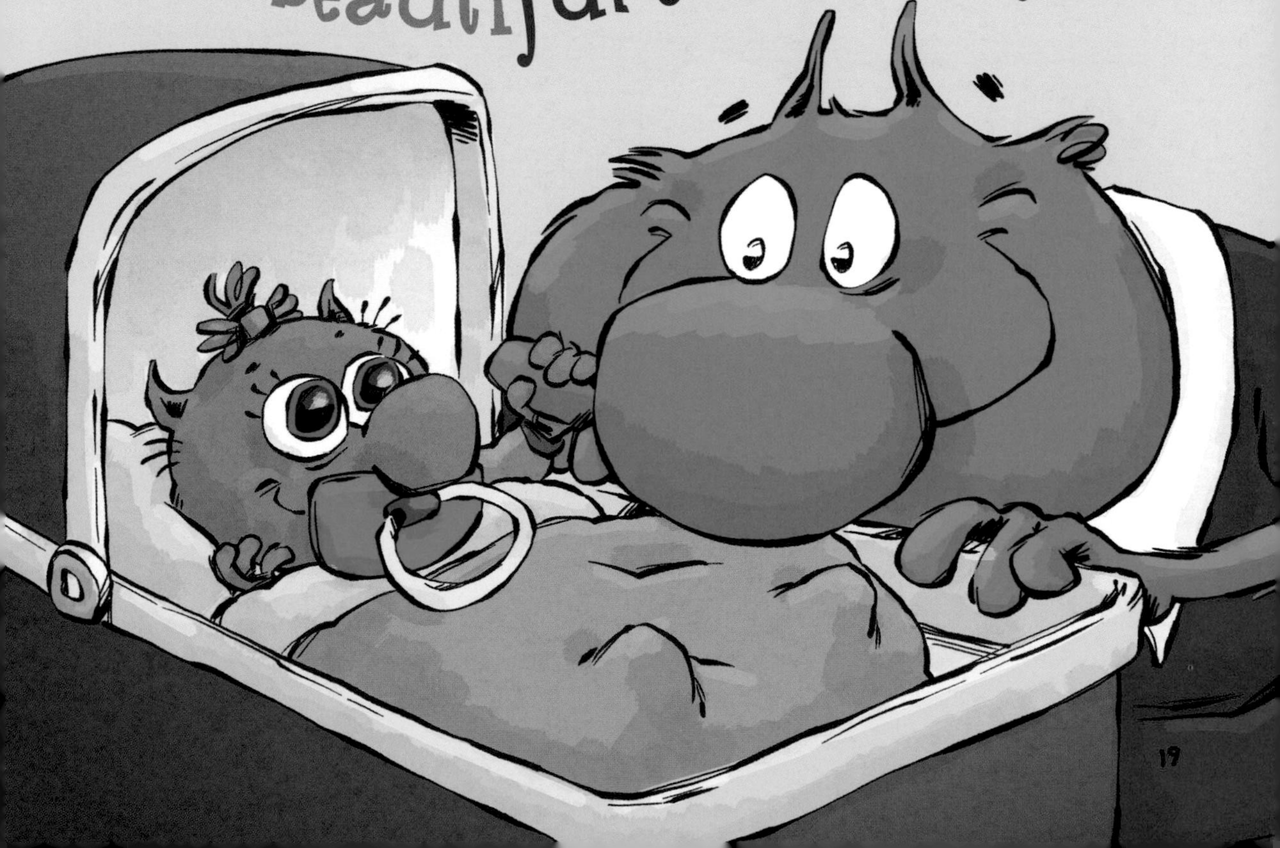

When L-Y is the suffix, it typically will tell

the way an action happens, as in "quickly, loudly yell!"

like "Good thing that's erasable.
She's writing on the table."

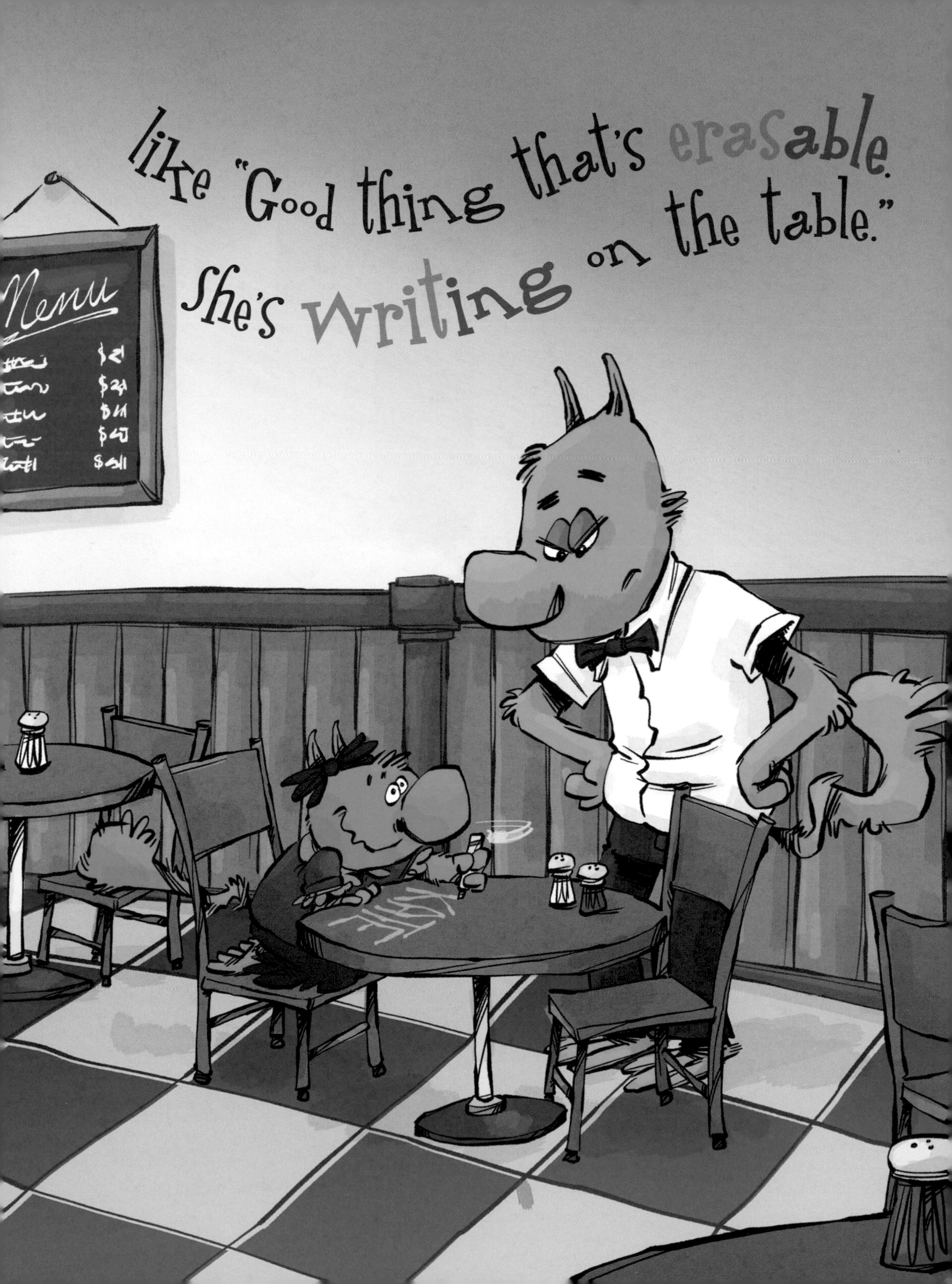

N–E–S–S often shows
a certain quality,

Like awkwardness and happiness and kindness, to name three.

Suffixes are all around!
Just look and you will see

Words like Jewish,
backWard, bluish,
fastest, slippery,

hairy, scary, voluntary,

neighborhood, advisement,

fearless, tearless, painful (ouch!),

creation, advertisement.

Knowing lots of these can build an excellent foundation—

and play a larger role in your amazing education!

So What is a Suffix?
Do you know?

SUFFIX	MEANING	EXAMPLE
-able	able to be	doable
-al	relating to; having to do with	herbal
-ary	of or relating to	secondary
-ed	past tense	transported
-er	a person who does an action	developer, reader
-er	more	browner, faster
-est	most	greatest
-ful	full of	useful, delightful
-hood	state, quality, or condition	childhood
-ing	action	singing
-ish	like or relating to	greenish, foolish
-ist	a person who does an action	artist
-ize	to cause or become	categorize, fantasize
-less	without	fearless
-ly	in a certain way	coldly, hungrily
-ment	action	movement
-ness	state or quality	shyness
-ous	full of	disastrous
-s	plural; more than one of	dolphins
-sion	state or quality	confusion
-tion	state or quality	complication
-y	made up of; characterized by	cheery

Find activities, games, and more at
www.brianpcleary.com

ABOUT THE AUTHOR AND THE ILLUSTRATOR
BRIAN P. CLEARY is the author of the best-selling *Words Are CATegorical*©
series as well as the *Math Is CATegorical*©, *Food Is CATegorical*™, *Animal Groups
Are CATegorical*™, *Adventures in Memory*™, and *Sounds Like Reading*© series. He
has also written *Do You Know Dewey? Exploring the Dewey Decimal System*,
Six Sheep Sip Thick Shakes: And Other Tricky Tongue Twisters, and several other
books. Mr. Cleary lives in Cleveland, Ohio.

MARTIN GONEAU is the illustrator of the *Food Is CATegorical*™ and *Animal
Groups Are CATegorical*™ series. Mr. Goneau lives in Trois-Rivières, Québec.

Millbrook Press
A division of Lerner Publishing Group, Inc.
241 First Avenue North
Minneapolis, MN 55401 USA

For reading levels and more information, look up this title at www.lernerbooks.com.

Main body text set in RandumTEMP 35/48. Typeface provided by House Industries.

Library of Congress Cataloging-in-Publication Data

Cleary, Brian P., 1959—
  -ful and -less, -er and -ness : what is a suffix? / By Brian P. Cleary ; Illustrations by Martin Goneau.
    pages cm. — (Words are CATegorical)
  ISBN 978-1-4677-0610-0 (lib. bdg. : alk. paper)
  ISBN 978-1-4677-2544-6 (EB pdf)
  1. English language—Suffixes and prefixes—Juvenile literature. 2. Language arts (Primary) I. Goneau,
Martin, illustrator. II. Title. III. Title: What is a suffix.
PE1175.C523 2014
428.1—dc23   2013017774

Manufactured in the United States of America
5-49657-12930-10/2/2020